Selecting Learning Experiences:
Linking Theory and Practice

Bruce R. Joyce

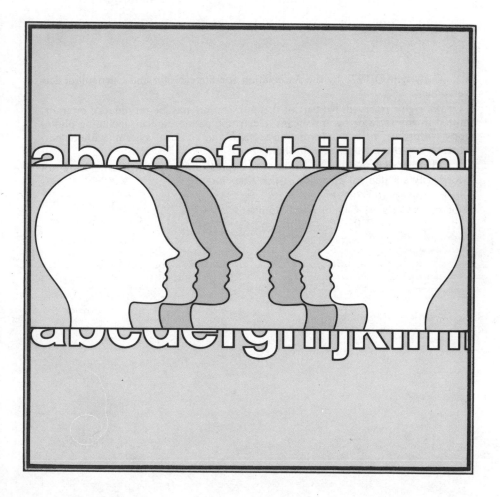

Association for Supervision and Curriculum Development
1701 K Street, N.W., Suite 1100
Washington, D.C. 20006

Stock number: 611-78138
Library of Congress Catalog Card Number: 78-60734
ISBN: 0-87120-091-0

Foreword

One of the most important, if not the most important, tasks of a teacher is selecting and creating an opportunity for a learning experience for his/her students. Too often in the past this process has been interpreted to mean the proper selection of materials to be used by the learner. This booklet does not follow the traditional interpretation, but creates a new direction by focusing on a matching relationship between teaching models and the learner's style of learning.

The author's three assumptions serve as a reminder to all of us in education of what we know about learning theories. The assumptions are: (a) there are a number of alternative approaches to teaching; (b) teaching methods make a difference in what is learned and how well it is learned; and (c) students are a powerful part of learning and react differently to each different teaching method.

Over 80 teaching strategies or models have been identified and categorized into four groups: (a) social interaction models; (b) information processing models; (c) personal models; and (d) behavior modification and cybernetic models. The author makes a case for student growth in each area and urges teachers to use models from each of the four groups.

This booklet is highly recommended for all teachers, supervisors, curriculum directors, department heads, and principals because it uses both theory and practice in the process of matching the student's learning style with the teaching model.

Donald R. Frost
President, 1978-79
Association for Supervision
and Curriculum Development

Introduction

In teaching, planning and doing are inextricably woven together. Planning is the selection of opportunities for learning experiences. Doing is creating experience in the classroom, working from but continuously modifying and adjusting the plans that are made prior to interacting with the students.

The focus of this paper is on the actions of the teacher in selecting and creating opportunities for learning experiences, and on a particular way of making available to teachers these products of theory and research that can enrich both the thinking and acting dimensions of teaching.

Thus, this paper rests on the belief that scholarship can enrich practice enormously. Through theory and research, we have built a variety of powerful and practical approaches to teaching (1). Many of these are not in wide use only because few practitioners have heard about them and have learned to use them. The science of education has been separated from practice by a gulf that is unnecessary and dysfunctional. Part of this gulf is a lack of information. The mechanisms simply have not been built that bring to teachers both a knowledge of theory and the skill to put it into action. Another reason is that theories have frequently not been made practical. Teachers by themselves have had to develop ways of managing children and carrying out instruction because scholars have failed to make theory and research as practical as it should and can be. However, there presently exists a large number of attractive theory-based models of teaching that have been developed to the point where they can be implemented in the practical world of the classroom. This reservoir of developed knowledge about teaching exists to the extent that we can now build bridges between the wisdom of practice and the strength of theory and research.

1

The concentration of this paper is on the selection of the process aspects of learning experience. We will not deal with curriculum or school organization, materials of instruction, or a variety of other important influences on the learning experience, although we will give some attention to content and materials. The important aspect is the identification of a storehouse of models of teaching, the purposes they are good for, and the process of applying them in the classroom to the selection of opportunities for learning experiences.

Curriculums, organizations, materials, and social contexts all profoundly influence what happens in the classroom, but the critical acts of selection and creation of process occur in or near the classroom and are the domain of the classroom teacher.

1.
A Point of View About Teaching

As teachers we are responsible for many types of instruction—helping our students grow in self-awareness and in their ability to relate to others, clarifying values, promoting moral development—the list is vast. All of these responsibilities can conveniently be described in three categories: (a) the personal growth of our students, including their feelings about self and development; (b) preparation for national and world citizenship; and, (c) mastery of academic subjects, including both the basic skills of reading and computation that are so essential to contemporary life; and (d) the most powerful findings of disciplined inquiry.

In order to accomplish these objectives, we work in schools, and within these in classrooms, learning centers, and libraries. Much of our contact with students is formal: They are assembled in classes, or learning teams to which teachers are assigned. Yet we have much informal contact with students. We work either relatively alone or in teaching teams, perhaps with paid and/or volunteer aides assisting us. As we work, we select and create opportunities for learning experiences for our students.

Our multiple responsibilities induce us to engage in several professional roles, often simultaneously. We are counselors, facilitators, instructional managers, curriculum designers, academic instructors, evaluators of instruction, and, reluctantly, disciplinarians.

Professional competence in teaching is an increased ability to fulfill these various roles effectively. A large part of this competence consists in mastering the repertoire of approaches to teaching appropriate to these roles. This competence is expanded in two ways: first, by increasing the *range of teaching strategies* that we are able to employ; second, by *becoming increasingly skillful* in the use of these strategies.

3

The Available Repertoire: Models of Teaching

There are presently available a considerable variety of teaching strategies that are based on defendable theories about how people learn, grow, and develop, and are designed to promote certain kinds of learning. For example, some are specially tailored to help students grow in self-awareness and strength of self-concept. Others were created to improve human relations in the classroom and helping students clarify their social values. Yet others are designed for the mastery of subject matter. Some are quite narrow in their focus, while others are useful for a wide variety of purposes. Some are quite formal. Others are casual and emergent.

Models of teaching are guidelines for designing educational activities and environments. They specify ways of teaching and learning—the patterns for teaching strategies.

Models of teaching can be found in many sources. Educators, psychologists, sociologists, systems analysts, psychiatrists, and many others have developed positions about learning and teaching. In addition, curriculum development projects, schools and school districts, and organizations representing particular curriculum areas or disciplines have generated approaches to teaching and learning. In preparing the most recent edition of the book, *Models of Teaching* (1), we identified more than 80 distinct models of teaching, far more than any teacher would be able to master during a career, each one grounded in a rationale or theory and clearly enough defined to be of practical use.

2.
Families of Models

Although each has distinctive features and purposes, Models of Teaching can be divided into four families whose members share a point of view about teaching and learning.

1. *Social Interaction Models.* (See Table 1.) These emphasize the relationships of the individual to society or to other persons. They focus on the processes by which reality is socially negotiated. Consequently, with respect to goals, models from this orientation give priority to the improvement of

Table 1. Social-Interaction Models—A Selection

Model	Major Theorist	Mission or Goals for Which Intended
Group Investigation	Herbert Thelen (2) John Dewey (3)	Development of skills for participation in democratic social process through combined emphasis on interpersonal (group) skills and academic inquiry skills. Aspects of personal development are important outgrowths of this model.
Social Inquiry	Byron Massialas (4) Benjamin Cox	Social problem-solving, primarily through academic inquiry and logical reasoning.
Laboratory Method	National Training Laboratory (NTL)(5) Bethel, Maine	Development of interpersonal and group skills and, through this, personal awareness and flexibility.
Jurisprudential	Donald Oliver (6) James P. Shaver	Designed primarily to teach the jurisprudential frame of reference as a way of thinking about and resolving social issues.
Role Playing	Fannie Shaftel (7) George Shaftel	Designed to induce students to inquire into personal and social values, with their own behavior and values becoming the source of their inquiry.
Social Simulation	Sarene Boocock (8)	Designed to help students experience various social processes and realities and to examine their own reactions to them.

the individual's ability to relate to others, to engage in democratic processes, and to work productively in the society. It must be stressed that the social-relations orientation does not assume that these goals constitute the *only* important dimension of life. While social relations may be emphasized more than other domains, social theorists are also concerned with the development of the mind and the self, and the learning of academic subjects. (It is the rare educator who is not concerned with more than one aspect of the learner's development or who does not use more than one aspect of the environment to influence the learner's development.)

2. *Information-Processing Models.* (See Table 2.) The second large family of models share an orientation toward the information processing capability of students and ways they can improve their ability to master information. Information-processing refers to the ways people handle stimuli from the environment, organize data, sense problems, generate concepts and solutions to problems, and employ verbal and nonverbal symbols. Some information-processing models are concerned with the ability of the learner to solve problems and thus emphasize productive thinking; others are concerned with general intellectual ability. A large number emphasize concepts and information derived from the academic disciplines. Again, however, it must be stressed that nearly all models from this family are also concerned with social relationships and the development of an integrated, functioning self. The route chosen, however, is through intellectual functioning.

3. *Personal Models.* (See Table 3.) The third family share an orientation toward the individual and the development of selfhood. They emphasize the processes by which individuals construct and organize their

Table 2. Information Processing Models—A Selection

Model	Major Theorist	Mission or Goals for Which Intended
Inductive Thinking Model	Hilda Taba (9)	Designed primarily for development of inductive mental processes and academic reasoning or theory building, but these capacities are useful for personal and social goals as well.
Inquiry Training Model	Richard Suchman (10)	
Scientific Inquiry	Joseph J. Schwab (11) (also much of the Curriculum Reform Movement of the 1960s)	Designed to teach the research system of a discipline, but also expected to have effects in other domains (sociological methods may be taught in order to increase social understanding and social problem-solving).
Concept Attainment	Jerome Bruner (12)	Designed primarily to develop inductive reasoning, but also for concept development and analysis.
Cognitive Growth	Jean Piaget (13) Irving Sigel (14) Edmund Sullivan (15)	Designed to increase general intellectual development, especially logical reasoning, but can be applied to social and moral development as well (see Kohlberg, 1966).
Advance Organizer Model	David Ausubel (16)	Designed to increase the efficiency of information processing capacities to meaningfully absorb and relate bodies of knowledge.
Memory	Jerry Lucas (17)	Designed to increase capacity to memorize.

Table 3. Personal Models—A Selection

Model	Major Theorist	Mission or Goals for Which Intended
Nondirective Teaching	Carl Rogers (18)	Emphasis on building the capacity for personal development in terms of self-awareness, understanding, autonomy, and self-concept.
Awareness Training	Fritz Perls (19) William Schutz (20)	Increasing one's capacity for self-exploration and self-awareness. Much emphasis on development of interpersonal awareness and understanding, as well as body and sensory awareness.
Synectics	William Gordon (21)	Personal development of creativity and creative problem-solving.
Conceptual Systems	David Hunt (22)	Designed to increase personal complexity and flexibility.
Classroom Meeting (Social Problem-Solving)	William Glasser (23)	Development of self-understanding and responsibility to oneself and one's social group.

unique reality. Frequently, they give much attention to emotional life. The focus on helping individuals to develop a productive relationship with their environments and to view themselves as capable persons is also expected to result in richer interpersonal relations and a more effective information processing capability.

4. *Behavior Modification and Cybernetic Models.* (See Table 4.) This fourth type of model has evolved from attempts to develop efficient systems for sequencing learning tasks and shaping behavior by manipulating reinforcement. Exponents of reinforcement theory, such as Skinner (24), have developed these models, and operant conditioning is their central mechanism. They are frequently referred to as behavior-modification theories because they emphasize changing the visible behavior of the learner rather than the underlying and unobservable behavior. Operant conditioning has been applied to a wide variety of goals, in education and other areas, ranging from military training to the improvement of interpersonal behavior and even to therapy. It is represented by a large number of models, some of which are media-oriented (such as programmed strategies and game-type

Table 4. Behavior Modification/Cybernetic Models—A Selection

Model	Major Theorist	Mission or Goals for Which Intended
Programmed Instruction	B. F. Skinner (24)	Facts, concepts, skills
Managing Behavior	B. F. Skinner (24)	Social behavior/skills
Relaxation	Rinn, Wolpe (25)	Personal goals (for example, reduction of stress, anxiety)
Anxiety Reduction	Rinn, Wolpe (25)	Substitution of relaxation for anxiety in social situations
Assertive Training	Wolpe (26)	Expression of feelings in social situation
Simulation	Link, Guetzkow (27)	Concepts and decision-making skills
Direct Training	Glaser (28) Lumsdaine (29)	Pattern of behavior, skills

simulations) and some of which are oriented to interactive teaching (such as the use of tokens to shape social behavior).

Common and Unique Features

These families of models are by no means antithetical or mutually exclusive, although each represents a distinctive approach to teaching. Whereas debates about educational method have seemed to imply that schools and teachers should choose one approach or another, students need growth in all areas. To tend the personal but not the social, or the informational but not the personal, and so on, simply does not make sense in the life of the growing student.

Hence, growth in teaching is the increasing mastery of a variety of models of teaching and the ability to use them effectively. Some philosophies of teacher education maintain that a teacher should master a single model and utilize it well. We believe that very few teachers are so limited in capacity. Most of us can quite easily develop a repertoire of six or eight models of teaching, which we can use in order to carry out our roles. We should choose our "basic" repertoire to meet the needs generated by our teaching assignment. Certain models are more appropriate for some curriculums than for others; that is, the curriculum helps define our role and the kinds of competencies that we need. (For example, a secondary school science teacher of biology who is using Biological Sciences Study Committee materials will want to master the particular kind of inductive approach that fits best with those materials. Or, a teacher of elementary school social studies who is helping children study values will want to master one of the models appropriate to clarifying values and analyzing public issues.)

Once a teacher masters the "basic" repertoire of models appropriate to his/her role, he or she can then expand it by learning new models and by combining and transforming the basic ones to create new ones. In the midst of a social studies unit, a teacher may use one model (for example, Inductive Thinking) to help children master map skills, and combine this model with group-dynamic models that help students attack social issues (for example, Group Investigation). A highly skilled performance in teaching blends the variety of models appropriately and embellishes them. Master teachers create new models of teaching and test them in the course of their work, drawing on the models of others for ideas that are combined in various ways.

In order to apply theories of learning to teaching, we need a basis from which we can reach into the storehouse of theoretical alternatives and select one approach. In the pages that follow, we will explore a position on learning and teaching that provides a foundation for the selection of teaching models.

3.
The Assumptive World That Links Theory and Practice

The position rests on several theses about the available models of teaching. *The first thesis is that there exists a considerable array of alternative approaches to teaching.* Many of these are practical and implementable in schools and classrooms where persons have the combination of skill and will. Further, these models of teaching are sufficiently different from one another that they change the probability that various kinds of outcomes will result if they are used. *Thus, the second thesis is that methods make a difference in what is learned as well as how it is learned.* The difference is probabilistic; particular methods boost certain outcomes and diminish others. Rarely do they guarantee some while obliterating the rest.

Third, *students are a powerful part of the learning environment, and students react differently to any given different teaching method.* Combinations of personality, aptitudes, interpersonal skills, and previous achievement contribute to configurations of learning styles so that no two people react in just the same way to any one model of teaching.

Operating from this stance, the task of the school and the teacher is to equip themselves with a basic variety of models of teaching that they can bring into play for different purposes, employ and adapt for different learners, and combine artfully to create classrooms and learning centers of variety and depth. To do this requires clarity about what models exist, what they can accomplish, and how different students will react to them.

Content and Method

Our focus in this paper is on *method* and learning style. The strength of the learner will be considered primarily in terms of the ways his/her

9

characteristics interact with the variety of models of teaching that are available. Content and instructional material are also important, however, because they, too, interact powerfully with teaching method. Content, obviously, is of enormous importance. In arithmetic, the emphasis given to algorithms, number facts, mathematical concepts, and problem solving can vary enormously from classroom to classroom, and selection from among the options within any content area enormously defines the opportunity to learn. In some physical education departments, soccer as a sport is available. In others, it is not. Some physics courses are slanted toward the applied, while others emphasize the theoretical. In literature courses, different weights can be given to poetry, short stories, and grammar, and different types of criticism can be emphasized. The continuous selection of content is an important function of teaching.

Similarly, materials have a powerful effect on the learning environment. In reading, for example, some teachers use a basal text without supplementary workbooks. Some teach through trade books with the children choosing what they will learn from. Other teachers build reading and language lessons from social studies and science materials. The materials themselves differ in structure and form. Audiovisual materials have properties vastly different from print materials and concrete objects.

Content and material for carrying content provide the raw, sensory data out of which learning is made. Teaching method transforms content and material through emphasis and process, and both vary according to the model that is used. For example, some models of teaching emphasize values —they highlight the value implications of the content. Other models emphasize the retention of factual material. Still others emphasize concepts or methods of inquiry. Thus, the selection of method magnifies certain aspects of content and diminishes others.

Process and Social Climate

The process of any method that is used is also learned to some degree. Models that are based on ways of inquiring teach methods of thinking as well as the content that is mastered. In other words, the method itself is learned by the student as he or she practices learning in that way.

Finally, a model of teaching creates a certain social system within the classroom, and this social system is learned as well. Properly implemented models based on democratic process create a democratic social system and require students to learn the skills of negotiation. Those emphasizing competition provide competitive social systems that are experienced and learned by the student. Thus, method defines the emphasis given to content, provides a process to be learned, and provides a social climate that will greatly influence the behavior of learners toward one another, toward the teacher, and will in the future affect his/her behavior toward others. The effects of method, thus, are complex and multidimensional.

Similarities and Differences in Process and Purpose

When we compare several models of teaching we find that the degree of differences among them varies quite a bit. Some models resemble each other in process, others in the social climates they generate, and still others in the content that is emphasized. By the same token, some are quite different in one or another of these aspects.

Very few models are good for one purpose only, although there are a few special purpose models. Most have a primary purpose and one or more secondary purposes. We speak of the primary directions as the *instructional* effects of a model and the secondary directions as their *nurturant* effects (31). The picture is complex because many models can be directed toward a variety of purposes. Thus, selecting a model is not always synonymous with the selection of purpose.

Synectics is an example (32). It was constructed to boost creative thinking. However, it can be applied to a number of content areas (science, social problems, creative writing, and so on). Group investigation, non-directive teaching, and behavior modification are appropriate for parts of nearly every subject area.

Also, models are seldom used alone for long periods of time.

Courses, units of work, learning centers, and curriculums generally require a combination of models. It is my opinion that there are very few models of teaching that are sufficient to define an entire curriculum, although one can serve as the core. Most models can be strengthened by combining them with a variety of others, both in order to be more effective in achieving any given set of desired learning outcomes, but also to increase stimulation and variety.

Effects can be increased by an artful pyramiding of the power of several models. For example, inductive thinking (Taba) can be strengthened by adding creativity training (Gordon) and inquiry training (Suchman).

Almost any process, however attractive at first, becomes less exciting after repeated usage unless variety is provided within it. Models offer to teachers the opportunity through blending to increase the variety and sustain the intensity of a course or unit, curriculum or learning center.

Thus, *the entire approach rests on the thesis that teachers can learn to select and blend models of teaching in such a way as to increase learning of various types. Various models can produce more of certain kinds of learning, and blends or combinations can increase the probability of increasing learning even more.*

Putting the Learner into the Equation

An important component of the position is that the style of the learner interacts with the characteristics of each model.

This cuts two ways. Not everyone reacts the same to any given method, and everyone reacts somewhat differently to different methods.

A variety of researchers have attempted to clarify the interaction between learner and method. The long-time work of Cronbach and Snow on seeking for aptitude treatment interactions (33) has attempted to bring some definition into the interaction of students with environments of various kinds. Hunt has adapted Kurt Lewin's old formula (behavior = person × environment) to approach the problem afresh by defining the types of learner characteristics that will affect and be affected by training methods that have different properties (34). Spaulding's definition of learning styles is accompanied by a set of hypotheses about the kinds of prescriptions that teachers can offer students who differ in important aspects of coping ability (35).

We can think of learning styles in two classes. *Generic styles* are important in helping us choose which models are most appropriate for various learners. They also provide guidelines for adapting and tailoring models to fit students' personalities. *Model specific styles* help us determine the reaction that any given student will have to one particular model or type of model. An example of generic styles is conceptual flexibility. (See Hunt (22).)

The less flexible students prefer models of high structure, which provide them with clear guidelines for behavior. The more conceptually complex individuals can adapt well to many models, but show a preference for those that provide them with the opportunity to contribute structure. An example of model-specific style is creativity. Creativity is directly relevant to models such as synectics, which are designed to improve divergent thinking directly. Highly creative individuals are likely to respond very differently to such a model than are students who rarely display creative ability. Similarly, sociability is likely to affect group process models of teaching. The more sociable students are likely to manifest a very different dynamic than are those students who are more withdrawn.

Three additional points about learning styles should be made. First, there is no knowledge base for a complete system for explicitly sorting students into categories that we might call "model appropriate." Very few, if any, students can profit from *only* one model of teaching. What is important is that some students will be more productive in some environments than in others, and this needs to be taken into account when designing their diet of learning experiences.

Second, it should be remembered that models are not fixed-formulas for learning environments. They can be adapted in structure, complexity, and by skill-training to help students relate to them. A model that provides little structure can be adapted to provide support for those learners who would be uncomfortable with an extremely low degree of prescription in their learning activities. Also, the task-complexity of models can be boosted or reduced in order to increase the student's capability or comfort with the model. Third, and perhaps most important, is that students can learn the skills necessary to help them increase their ability to profit from most models. In a series of studies, Hunt and Joyce and their associates found that students whose conceptual levels were matched and mismatched with several models of teaching learned different amounts and types of content and process. They also found that it was possible to teach mismatched students some of the behaviors necessary to increase their participation in the mismatched model. If this was true for students selected for extremes of match and mismatch of various models (as in the Hunt-Joyce studies), the odds are that it will hold for students more in the center of distribution.

Thus, the characteristics of the learner are relevant to the selection of learning experiences in three ways. First, they provide us with a basis for identifying those models with which students will be most and least comfortable. Second, they provide us with guidelines by which we can adapt models of teaching so that they will be more productive for students. Third, they provide guidelines for locating the skills students need to get the most profit from particular models of teaching.

4.
The Effects of Method Are Relative

At times it is argued that teaching methods are completely different with respect to their power.

This is probably not the case. Each one is likely to boost certain kinds of learning for specific kinds of learners, but most have positive effects on several kinds of learning.

Models are not like a series of interchangeable parts that have different effects so that we can plug one in and get one effect, another for another effect, and so on. It is rather that each one increases the likelihood that students will learn certain kinds of things, but does not depress other learning outcomes.

The Learner Does the Learning

To begin with, it is the student who does the learning and is the most powerful person in the teaching/learning situation. Intelligence, adaptability, creativity, motivation, and general configurations of personality are much more important determiners of how much the student will learn than anything the teacher or curricular system can do. Given the opportunity to learn certain kinds of material, his/her capability will more determine what will result than will anything else. Teaching, however, can boost the likelihood that he/she will develop in certain kinds of ways, and effective teaching can be very powerful if all of the teachers in a given school are devoted to the achievement of certain kinds of learning outcomes, such as creativity, and select models oriented toward creative thinking. The odds are increased that the learners will become more creative in the long run. However, the students will continue to learn facts, concepts, interpersonal skills, and so on.

15

Learning Objectives Overlap, Too

The world would be much simpler if learning objectives did not over-lap, if we sought only one at a time, and if models of teaching were com-pletely objective specific. In that case, we could generate a clean matrix and say, "If you want to accomplish objective X, use method X." However, life is not so simple. Various kinds of objectives not only overlap, but turn out in many cases to be embedded in one another. Also, we rarely seek one objective at a time. For example, consider some of the objectives of primary grade reading. The objective of increasing students' word attack skills does not stand alone. It also relates to comprehension. Also, a stu-dent's love of reading and understanding of what reading is used for probably affects the development of skills. Additionally, in every lesson, we are trying to help the student feel better as a reader and as a person. Finally, in every unit the teacher is helping a group of children to work together effectively as learners. That which appears at first to be a simple enough class of objectives—increasing one's ability to sound out words having certain kinds of characteristics—turns out to overlap with other objectives and is not an objective we would pursue in disregard of a variety of others. Consequently, as we select a model, we want to choose one that will have a good chance of achieving not only the objective which happens to be the substantive core of the lesson of the moment (boosting word attack skills in this case), but which also will be likely to pay off and not interfere with the other kinds of learning that are associated with it.

Any set of objectives is generally weighted in terms of general importance, and the weights vary from time to time. Helping the student achieve a positive self-concept has a large valence for some of us and a moderate valence for others. At certain times, we concentrate heavily on helping children to work together, whereas in other cases that objective is less prominent. Fortunately, most models of teaching are likely to produce more than one kind of learning at any given time. Counseling methods were derived to help the student understand him/herself and become an independent well-integrated personality and learner, but they can also be used to teach reading or almost any other subject. Ausubel's theory of verbal learning (36), which gives rise to the advanced organizer model of teaching, is designed to increase the mastery of verbal material by providing the students with sets of concepts (an intellectual scaffolding) within which they can store new material. Yet that model teaches the concepts that are at the core of the academic disciplines—as well as facilitating the retention of verbal material, and it also implicitly encourages a certain attitude toward the nature of subject matter and what school learning is.

Models of teaching can be modified and adapted so as to increase the likelihood that they will boost certain kinds of learning. For example, role playing, which is designed to make personal values accessible for study, can be combined with counseling approaches to provide intellectual grist for the mill and help students acquire a strategy for analyzing values. Thus, the problem of selection is one of identifying the multiple learning objectives and determining which models are most likely, with any given group of students or individual student, to boost the objectives most fervently sought, knowing that others will be reached as well.

On Adding, Blending, and Not Being Heavy-Handed

The power of any given model of teaching is relative to any other model (and affected by the style of the learner as well). Even when one model is clearly the most powerful with respect to any objective that is being sought, one may not necessarily select that model at any given time because another model boosts other objectives that deserve some priority or because a different model will reach the learner more clearly and effectively.

For example, a ski instructor may use very direct instructional models that focus on the building of skills. However, the instructor also hopes that the students will continue to instruct themselves, gradually overcome their fear of the mountain, and gradually develop the spontaneity and integratedness of movements that make specific skills almost imperceptible from one another. Thus, at certain times, the instructor may use methods more like those described in "Inner Tennis" (37) or "Inner Skiing" (38), which are designed to help the student "feel" the sport and free him/her from the constraints of fear, a self-image of awkwardness, and an overemphasis on performing individual skills in isolation from one another.

Teaching method is often debated as if given methods were in opposition to one another. This is rarely the case. I am extremely suspicious of "overadvocacy" of any given method even for a very specific purpose. One of the great teachers of tennis, Vic Braden (39), operates a tennis college that, on the surface, would appear to be very skill-oriented. He uses a model in which tennis skills are modeled both on film and in person by instructors. Students receive television feedback, and practice is given with ball machines that shoot several hundred balls an hour at the trainee. When teaching persons how to play doubles, however, Braden does not rely solely on the training models, for doubles is a matter of cooperation and mutual confidence. A good doubles team has to coordinate not only on an intellectual level, but on a level that is built out of rapport. Braden takes great pains to teach rapport and to help his students understand what harm disintegrative behaviors, such as deprecating one's partner, do to the team. The training model is clearly the most used and relied on, but there are strong elements of counseling and something of the atmosphere of a very lighthearted "T-group" in his approach to doubles. Nearly everyone, regardless of his/her level of tennis, comes away from the tennis college feeling good about himself/herself.

Thus it is with academic subjects. Some instructors so overuse mastery models of learning that their students become sick of the subject they are being taught. When I was in high school, I was one of the poorest members of a good swimming team. The coach used drill-and-practice methods to teach us the strokes and how to increase our speed. He was tremendously encouraging to all of us, including those who really were not doing the team that much good. We loved him, enjoyed each other, and felt good about ourselves. As my body matured in college, I showed some promise as a long-distance swimmer and was taken under the wing of a fairly genial but hard-driving coach who emphasized practice rather than instruction. Given the academic demands of college, our little group had keys to the pool and were asked to swim for four to six hours sometime during each evening or night. It was, of course, not his fault that he couldn't be there to provide variety, but one of the side-effects of that experience is that I have not swum five consecutive laps since I was 20 years old. I love to play in the water, but I have an incredible aversion to anything remotely resembling swimming practice. One should not overgeneralize this, of course; beyond skills of a certain level, sports are incredibly demanding of one's tolerance for practice in boredom.

What is true in athletics is also true in the academic classroom. Even the most skilled use of models to help us inquire into English literature needs to be leavened by playful, enjoyable, and spontaneous reading without analytic overtones. On the other hand, if the only English instruction received were loose and playful, the students would be shortchanged by not developing the concepts and tools of analysis that are essential for a full comprehension of the subject. Thus, balance is important, and the arts of teaching require delicacy and restraint. Even though particular models of teaching will generally boost certain kinds of learning outcomes, they can be run into the ground with heavy-handedness or overuse.

In addition, the teachers' comfort with certain models will influence their effectiveness. Although a professional teacher has no excuse for not continuously struggling to improve his/her repertoire, there are certain approaches with which the teacher will be most comfortable or simply enjoy tremendously. Within limits, one should relax and use what is most natural and spontaneous. A good group-dynamics teacher can learn to blend in techniques from other models that will help the students to master subject matter and learn tools of inquiry. The staple approach may be through group process augmented by other models that at first do not "feel as natural." Similarly, a good academic instructor can gradually learn tools of counseling and group dynamics to balance the teacher process.

Specific models can also have a particular personal appeal for short-term use. When I am working with my classes, there are certain days when I simply have a terrific urge to get things clarified or when I want to express myself and the way I think about material. On those days, I am very likely to lecture with the use of advance organizers. There are other days when I would be bored silly by that same approach, and use another to stay lively and help the students stay with me. Pretending that we are not people would be a serious error in teaching, and our intuition about what feels right on any given day should be listened to, even though we select models on an analytic basis much of the time.

5.
The Probable Effects of Models of Teaching

As stated earlier, each of the families of Models of Teaching comes from a somewhat different view of humankind and how he/she learns, and they are weighted toward certain priorities. Within any of the families, however, there are models that have been used for virtually any of the purposes that are the primary focus of the other families. The difference is a matter of emphasis and degree.

There is no body of research that compares the range of models of teaching with respect to the spectrum of educational objectives. There is a vast body of research about single models and a substantial body comparing two or three models with respect to two or three classes of objectives. However, the accumulated empirical findings do not begin to constitute a complete cross/models—cross/objectives matrix.

Nonetheless, from the intra-model research and the orientation of the models, we can justify statements about the probable relative effects of each family and the specific boosts to learning that are likely from the individual models.

Models, Missions, and Objectives

There are three types of missions in education:

1. We can attempt to reach the learner through the academic domain, by teaching academic skills and ways of dealing intellectually with the complexity of the world (as, for example, an attempt to teach mathematics). Information Processing and Cybernetic Models were developed for this purpose.

2. We can attempt to improve the capacity of the learner through intervention in the personal domain (as through an attempt to increase student self-direction). Personal Models were developed for this purpose.

21

3. We can attempt to enter the social domain, to change the learner at the point of interaction with his/her fellows (as when an attempt is made to teach social or economic skills). Social Models were developed to accomplish this.

Point of Entry: The Strategy of the Scholar

Focuses that originate in the academic disciplines are characterized by the attempt to intervene in the life of the student by teaching ideas and techniques that have been developed by scholars. Probably more schools use academic content as their point of entry than any other approach. Mathematics is taught with the belief that the mathematician's ways of thinking and calculating will be useful in the life of the learner. History, or the historian's way of thinking, is taught with the hope that the sweep of history will help the growing student orient himself/herself in the flow of humanity. Content from the sciences is taught, or less frequently, the systems of thinking employed by scientists are introduced, to help the child learn the technologies of the modern world. Still less frequently, aesthetics, ethics, and humanitarian philosophies are taught to the child. More often than those, foreign languages, literature, or the social sciences are explored, although none of these is common in American public schools. (See Table 6.)

The accumulated knowledge of the human race is increasingly concentrated in the hands of professional scholars. In the humanities, sciences, and social sciences, knowledge is produced systematically and at an explosive rate. And many pursuits that were at first the result of the practical imagination of human beings (such as marine architecture and agriculture) have become the objects of systematic scholarship. The larger universities presently include people studying just about every conceivable human activity.

The school is the first formal link between this scholarly activity and the child. It can function to make the scholarly world accessible to the child and to prepare him/her for a lifelong relationship to scholarly material.

In the view of many people, the school should find its primary functions in the academic domain. Some of these people simply see academic learning as the route to all development in all domains—they tend to brand any other function as "anti-intellectual" and therefore bad. Others, however, are increasingly concerned with the complexity of the modern world and the need for every person who can to be able to handle this complexity conceptually. They too see the organized scholarly disciplines as the best possible source of this knowledge.

Far and away, the most common performance goal in education is to transmit the technical and symbolic systems that we use to communicate.

That is to say, reading, writing, and arithmetic receive the greatest emphasis in today's elementary schools. The nursery, kindergarten, and primary school years especially, spanning from age three or four to about nine, are devoted almost exclusively to language and number development. In the middle grades, we find map skills, study skills, information-location techniques, summary writing, and the like. In secondary schools, the emphasis shifts to learning symbol systems of the various areas of knowledge, so that the technical language of biology, mathematics, or grammar can be more precisely utilized.

The fact that the technical-symbolic performance goal is so well established and so likely to be agreed on as one of the missions of the schools encourages the author to minimize a discussion of it here—to spare the reader what he or she already knows. In general, that goal emphasizes precise mastery of reading, mathematics, writing, and the skills necessary to handle material in the academic areas.

Table 6. Alternate Objectives Within the Academic Domain

1. Emphasize general symbolic proficiency (reading, writing, arithmetic, technical skills).
2. Emphasize information from selected disciplines (history, geography, literature, and so on).
3. Emphasize major concepts from the disciplines.
   a. Treat broad, related fields together (social studies, language, arts, science).
   b. Treat a few disciplines separately (economics, physics, history, music).
4. Emphasize modes of inquiry (ways of thinking) of the disciplines.
5. Emphasize broad philosophical schools or problems (aesthetics, humanitarian issues, ethics).

When playing the role of instructional manager, the teacher emphasizes symbolic proficiency or competence. When playing the role of inquiry trainer, the teacher can take any of the last four emphases, depending on the curriculum plan within which she/he is operating, the children with whom she/he is working, and the preference she/he shares with fellow teachers.

Point of Entry: Personal Capacity

The human organism has many potential capacities for responding to its environment. There is intelligence, which includes the ability to solve problems, to analyze and synthesize information and to build new ideas. There is creativity, or the capacity to take the environment and do new and interesting things with it. There is the organization of the inner self, the feeling of adequacy or openness, and the ability to grow and to face complexity. There is independence or autonomy, the capacity to respond fearlessly and on one's own terms. There are feelings of warmth and affiliation, which enable a comfortable and nonthreatening response. (See Table 7.)

In the role of counselor, the teacher tries to increase these capacities. He or she may emphasize creativity, for example, and do everything possible to teach students to make a creative, aesthetic response to life. Or activities may be organized around the attempt to increase intelligence and rationality. Or the focus may be on means of increasing the personality development of the individual.

A school that sees its mission as the development of personal capacity will emphasize the individual in everything it does, and thus, emphasize the role of person-seeker for all of its teachers. The school will try to challenge pupils, to free them, to teach them how to teach themselves. Such a school will concentrate on the personal capacity of the individual and subordinate attention to social and academic demands in favor of personal roles.

Table 7. Alternate Objectives Within the Personal Domain

1. The developing organization of the self
2. The development of productive thinking capacity (including creativity, flexibility, ability to produce alternatives)
3. The development of a personal meaning
4. The development of self-teaching and problem-solving ability
5. The development of aesthetic capacity
6. The development of motivation to achieve

The Developing Organization of the Self. In recent years, a large number of educators and psychologists, many of them from schools of humanistic and personal psychology, have believed that a central mission of education should be the development of a strong self, the creation of a person who feels adequate and who reaches out warmly and integratively to others. These theorists believe that the function of the school lies in helping the child find and develop a healthy self, one with great capacity for personal and social development (40). Education should help the child find direction rather than impose it on him or her.

The Development of Productive Thinking Capacity. Creative problem-solving—the ability to produce alternatives and/or the capacity to integrate material into new forms—could be the means of allowing the individual to find new routes to self-fulfillment. Theorists like Torrance, Taylor, and Thelen have seen creative thinking as the central purpose of the school. Psychologists like Hunt, Torrance, Rokeach, and Wertheimer have studied the characteristics of creativity and the kinds of environments that stimulate it (41).

The Development of a Personal Meaning. Other theorists have emphasized the capacity to discover personal meaning in life and to avoid alienation through affiliation with humankind. Writers like Fromm, Phenix, and Linser (42) have described the process by which persons discover themselves and find meaning in a social world. In so doing, they have defined another possible goal for the school.

The Development of Self-teaching and Problem-solving Ability. Another avenue is to attempt to increase the student's capacity to direct his or her own learning, to solve problems independently, and to plan and organize independent lines of inquiry. This emphasis is found in the writing of Dewey, Holt, Hullfish and Smith, and Miel, among others (43). Supporters of this goal assume that the self-directed individual will continue to grow and seek self-fulfillment throughout life.

The Development of Aesthetic Capacity. Quite a different objective is to try to affect the students' aesthetic capacities—to change their response to beauty in the world and to imbue them with the drive to enhance the beauty in their lives and their physical and social environments. In the works of Ducasse, Beittel, Eisner, Santayana, and again, Dewey, this approach is found.

The Development of Motivation To Achieve. Another distinct approach is to try to arouse the student's desire for self-improvement, the desire to master knowledge and skills. Described by the psychologists McClelland and Atkinson (44), among others, this approach is recommended by educators like Hansen and can be seen in the philosophy of many of the programs of compensatory education. Such programs frequently try to arouse the desire of inner-city children to develop themselves more fully.

These are six of the possible alternative objectives that can give focus to the role of person seeker. All of the six probably sound like worthy ends to the reader. Any of the six would serve nobly as the driving mission of a fairly vigorous school or classroom. Yet these are only a few of the possible focuses of the role.

Point of Entry: Social Interaction

Teachers can seek, in their roles as group leaders, to enter the learners' lives in such a way as to directly affect their relations with groups, the society, and the culture. The school can help commit the student to a life of service and social activism. There are schools, for instance, where the children are involved in social work from the middle elementary years and where many of them take part in political activities and the affairs of international organizations. These activities reflect the focus of those schools on developing the social commitment of the students. The works of Kenworthy, Preston, and Cahm (45), describe such a goal.

Cooperative Problem Solving. Another societal focus was recommended by Dewey, who saw the school committing the student to the cooperative problem-solving method. The school would be operated as a miniature democracy in which the young citizens would learn the arts of cooperative inquiry and would apply the scientific method to the problems that interested them as individuals and that confronted them as social beings. While Dewey was the most formal and thorough spokesman of this view, it is also found today, though in quite different forms, in the works of Thelen, Miel, Michaelis, and others (46). Recently, this has been expressed as an emphasis on social activism in some of the experimental schools of Washington, D.C., and other large cities.

Economic Competence. Another objective in the social domain might be the development of economic independence. The school might emphasize the skills and knowledge that are essential for economic survival and development. This is a more common mission for technical junior and senior high schools than it is for elementary schools, but many people see reading and arithmetic as the central elementary school "subjects" because of their potential economic usefulness.

Nationalism. In the schools of many nations, there have been attempts to dominate the social education of the child with a commitment to the nationalistic ends. In William L. Shirer's *The Rise and Fall of the Third Reich*, there is an excellent description of the program to induct the youth of Germany during the 1930s into the service of the state. The nationalistic emphasis, in less extreme forms, still exists in schools (47).

Human Relations. Another approach to social education is to attempt to improve human relations directly. Such a mission characterized the school improvement program of the Wilmington, Delaware, public schools in the late 1950s and early 1960s under the direction of Muriel Crosby (48). The philosophy of the Bank Street School (49) also reflected this emphasis.

The possible ways of approaching the student at the point of interaction with society are as numerous as the ways of mounting an attempt to develop personal ability. And, of course, personal and social development can and should be seen together. The attempt, for example, to develop a creative response might be combined with a focus on thinking creatively with respect to the society. Similarly, the attempt to focus on personal problem-solving ability might be combined with a focus on cooperative problem-solving.

The approach to personality development outlined by psychologists Harvey, Hunt, and Schroder describes the intellectual capacity to deal with complexity simultaneously with the capacity to handle interpersonal relations. Hence, their structure integrates a way of looking at intellectual and interpersonal complexity together (50).

In sum, educational objectives can be divided into the personal, social, and academic with the understanding that the categories are seen as avenues and are not mutually exclusive. Personal growth, for example, can lead to academic growth. Most schools will seek to enter in all three areas. Table 9 summarizes the objectives that have been discussed here.

The array of broad goals is considerable. When described in terms of specific objectives, the number becomes vast. Fortunately, the available array of approaches to teaching is muscular—there are more than enough methods to use even for such a complex of purposes.

Table 8. Alternative Objectives Within the Social Domain

1. Enculturation: socializing the child to a culture and transmitting a cultural heritage.
2. Developing competence as an international citizen.
3. Developing cooperative problem-solving capacity (democratic-scientific approach, political and social activism).
4. Developing economic competence and social mobility.
5. Promoting nationalistic fervor.
6. Improving human relations: increasing affiliation and decreasing alienation.

Table 9. Selected Missions of Education

Missions:	Academic Skills	Personal Capacity	Social Interaction
Alternative Objectives:	1. Information from selected disciplines (commonly history, geography, and literature)	1. Self-organization	1. Enculturation
	2. Structure of knowledge (concepts from disciplines)	2. Productive thinking	2. Internationalism
	3. Modes of inquiry (how scholars think)	3. Personal meaning	3. Cooperative problem-solving and social activism
	4. Broad philosophical school or problems (aesthetics, ethics, and so on)	4. Self-teaching and problem-solving	4. Economic competence
	5. Technical-symbolic skills (reading, arithmetic)	5. Aesthetic capacity	5. Nationalism
		6. Motivation to achieve	6. Human relations: affiliation v. alienation

The Probable Effects of Families of Models of Teaching

The families of models of teaching have distinctive orientations that lend themselves to particular clusters of missions. *However, it should not be assumed that the families are tailored only for specific domains of objectives. Personal models, for example, can be employed to achieve social and academic goals.* The issue of selection is one of relative emphasis and suitability for the learner.

Personal Models

The emphasis is on the unique character of each human being and the struggle to develop as an integrated, confident, and competent personality. The goal is to help each person to "own" his/her own development and to achieve a sense of self-worth and personal harmony. Personalists emphasize the integration of the emotional and intellectual selves.

They attempt to help the student understand himself/herself and his/her goals and to develop the means for educating himself/herself. Much reliance is placed on the student's self-understanding and helping him/her to become the active agent in learning. Many of the personal models of teaching have been developed by counselors, therapists, and other persons interested in the stimulation of individual creativity and self-expression. Motivation for learning comes from inside rather than outside, and these models are shaped to release the energy of the individual so that he/she can reach out to the knowledge that lies about in experiential and symbolic form. Knowledge is seen then as possessed by the individual and transformed by him/her. A unique frame of reference controls the nature of knowledge as it resides within the individual.

The mastery of academic content and skills is done by the individual. As the student understands himself/herself and reflects on his/her purposes and goals, he/she will reach out for development.

The teacher has to accept the student as one who is competent in self-direction. The teacher brings new ideas and interpersonal situations within range of the student, but trusts him/her to generate his/her own education with the help of a counselor, teacher, and fellow students. Teaching becomes helping the student to teach himself/herself. Thus, the primary goals are: (a) to increase the student's sense of self-worth; (b) to help the student understand himself/herself more fully; (c) to help the student contact his/her emotions and become more aware of the way emotions affect other aspects of behavior; (d) to help the student develop goals for learning; (e) to help the student develop plans for increasing competence; (f) to increase the student's creativity and playfulness; and (g) to increase the student's openness to new experience.

From these, the student with a counselor teacher reaches out to master academic content and skills. Thus, one can "teach" the goals toward the objectives of academic subjects, but it is through the learner and through the learner's cooperation that one teaches. The teacher's academic expertise becomes available to the learner because of their cooperative relationship. Together the learner and teacher plan to use other models of teaching, drawing on the resources for learning that have originated from other stances.

Thus, the personal models instruct the self and nurture the mastery of academic material.

Social Models

Social models draw on the energy of the group and capitalize both on common cause and the potential that comes from differing points of view and orientations. The core objective is to help the students to learn to work together to identify and solve problems. These may be academic or social in nature. Increasing ability in group organization, problem identification, clarification of values, and the development of social skills are primary goals. As in the case of the Personal Models, academic content and skills are developed as a part of the inquiry. Problems and values are the focus. The material is mastered in relation to them.

Some of the social family models are quite specific in their orientation (the Jurisprudential Model, for example, focuses on public issues and clarifying values in relation to those issues), but many of them are quite broad and can be used to approach almost any academic subject matter.

The primary goals are: (a) to help students work together to identify and solve problems; (b) skills in human relations; and (c) awareness of personal and social values. Secondary goals are derived from the direction of the group and can include the range of academic and social content.

The Information Processing Family

These focus directly on intellectual capability. Some work directly on the teaching and thinking, whereas others teach general or specific academic methods of inquiry, and still others facilitate the mastery of subject matter.

Information processing models can be either inductive, deductive, or what is called "guided" discovery. Inductive models pull the student through processes of inquiry. The student collects and analyzes data and is led to form concepts about it. Deductive models provide the student with frameworks for mastering subject matter and present the material to him/her. Guided discovery models lead the student step-by-step through a series of tasks that represent intellectual processes.

The primary purposes are: (a) the mastery of methods of inquiry; (b) the mastery of academic concepts and facts; and (c) the development of general intellectual skills, such as the ability to think more logically.

Since social and personal concerns can be the subject of intellectual inquiry, these models can also be used to nurture the development of social skills, understanding of values, and personal understanding.

Cybernetics and Behavior Modification

The essence of these approaches is that the human being is an information processing system that learns from getting feedback about the effects of behavior.

While both depend on feedback, the cybernetic approaches present the person with tasks, provide feedback, and help the person see the relationship between performance and the goals to be achieved. As the individual succeeds and errs, he/she will notice the consequences and will experiment with his/her behavior until a satisfactory level of performance is reached. Cybernetic approaches may or may not use external rewards, but if they do, the rewards come at the end of a series of tasks when a major skill or concept has been mastered, and the student generally is permitted to reward himself/herself. Behavior modification approaches depend on the establishment of a contingency schedule in which correct performance is approved immediately. Sometimes this is accomplished by the development of programmed tasks designed to ensure errorless performance under the assumption that knowledge of correct performance is satisfying and reinforcing in itself.

Cybernetic and behavior modification approaches have been applied to nearly the entire range of personal, social, and academic skills, including skills in the psychomotor domain.

The Probable Effects of Specific Models

Within the families, specific models have particular purposes (see Tables 1-4). Some are designed for *very* special purposes and have little general use (the Jurisprudential Model and the Relaxation Model are examples) while others, such as Group Investigation are very broad. Since there has been relatively little cross-model research, our data base for relative effects is slim, but research on specific models is generally positive. The ones described in Tables 1-4 generally achieve the purposes for which they are designed.

Table 10 depicts the probability that ten models of teaching will boost several classes of learning outcomes directly or nurturantly.

Table 10. Probable Outcomes Boosted by Ten Models of Teaching

MODELS (Family)		Self Understanding	Awareness	Creativity	Interpersonal Skills	Social Values	Academic Inquiry	Concepts	Factual Material	Academic Skills	Psychomotor Skills
Nondirective Teaching	P	D	N	N	V	V	N	N	N	N	N
Group Investigation	S	D	N	N	D	N	D	N	N	N	N
Synectics	P	N	N	D	D	N	N	N	N	N	N
Gestalt (Awareness Oriented)	P	D	D	N	D	D					
Advance Organizer	IP						N	D	D	N	
Inductive Thinking	IP						D	D	D	D	
Inquiry Training	IP						D	D	D	D	
Cybernetic (simulation)	CBM				V	V	V	D	D	D	D
Cybernetic (training)	CBM				D(V)	V	D	D	D	D	D
Behavior Modification	CBM	V			V		V	D	D	D	D

D = Direct (Primary)
N = Nurturant (Secondary)
V = Variable, Depending on Focus (Generally Nurturant)

The pattern of Table 10 indicates the relative breadth and narrowness of the direct and nurturant effects of several models of teaching. Most of the personal and social models are relatively specifically directed, but nurture a wide variety of learning objectives. The information processing models are directed toward a larger span of objectives, but chiefly function in the academic domain. Their nurturant effects are not as broad as the personal and social models. Generally speaking, personal and social models are more nurturant in character, and information processing, cybernetic, and behavior modification models are more directive. The probable cause for this is that those models that focus on the individual human being attempt not only to improve people's self-understanding and awareness, but also to help them develop in a wide variety of ways.

Nondirective teaching and group investigation are probably the broad-est of all models. The first, developed from the counseling orientation, attempts to help the individual develop across the spectrum of possibilities. Group investigation, deriving as it does from a concern with broad societal development and the development of the individual through the life of the group, also seeks to facilitate growth in many areas.

Selecting Learning Experiences

Keeping in mind that this is based on somewhat speculative reasoning and that the probable effects are relative, we have nonetheless arrived at the beginning of a clarified position from which to select and adapt models of teaching to increase the likelihood that various kinds of learning will take place. The position rests on the contention that there are real differ-ences among the approaches to teaching and that these differences have real effects on what is learned. Essentially, teaching is the creation of learning environments, and different environments are directed toward or nurture different kinds of learning.

If we add to that contention Hunt's reformulation of Lewin's maxim that behavior is a function of person X environment, then selected learning experiences are essentially a coordination of objectives, learner, and en-vironment.

Objectives provide definitions of the behavior and content to be sought. Except for the most minute "lesson" or teaching episode, there are usually multiple objectives, with degrees of priority attached to them. As illustrated earlier, a large scale unit of a course in reading includes a con-cern with skill, self-concept, and desire to read, among others. Thus, most complex units or courses require the use of several models.

Learners differ in myriad ways. Self-concept, achievement, personality, and cognitive development are but a few of the dimensions along which we can differentiate the people we teach. To complicate matters, differences among students are often not highly correlated. There are high achievers with poor self-concepts and extroverts with good self-concepts and terrible study skills. We want to tailor learning environments to fit the learner as closely as possible, but we have practical limitations. A simple formula is to translate student characteristics into two dimensions: a need for and tolerance of *structure,* and a need for and tolerance of *task complexity. Structure refers to the degree of prescription in the environment.* The greater the structure, the more detailed the plan, and the less independence is provided. Task complexity refers to the intricacy of the process—the more complex tasks require higher degrees of skill on the part of the learner.

Hunt suggests that we strive for an "optimal mismatch" between the present capacity of the learner and the model that is chosen so as to "pull" the student toward greater capacity, but not overstress his/her capabilities. Environments can also be modified to accommodate learner needs and/or model-relevant skills can be taught as necessary.

Hence, we can select models according to their appropriateness for the objectives we seek and their "fit" to learner preference for structure and varying degrees of task complexity. Compromise is obviously necessary. Nondirective teaching, for example, is appropriate for the objective of improving self-esteem, but may be too unstructured for some learners. Higher structures may be introduced or a different model, such as Awareness Training, might be used because it is targeted similarly, but can easily be employed with a fair amount of structure.

The Personal, Social, and Information Processing models of teaching roughly correspond to personal, social, and academic missions, but as indicated earlier, the correspondence is not of the one-to-one variety. It is a question rather of emphasis and the extent to which objectives are pursued directly or nurtured. Also, as indicated earlier, we would seldom use a single model of teaching alone, but rather would use combinations to boost the effects of one another and also modify them to reach learners who need different degrees of task complexity and structure. A complete discussion of the selection of models appropriate to various objectives and learner characteristics requires a rather complete knowledge of a large number of models, something that cannot be accomplished in a short paper. The models mentioned in Tables 2 to 4 represent the capability to boost learning in nearly every domain and are characterized by a large range of degrees of structure and task complexity. Among them, they can reach nearly every learner. Careful selection should increase the probability of reaching nearly every learner in such a way as to boost the desired kinds of learning.

Table 11. Models or Strategies: Selected Studies

Patricia D. Murphy. "Training in Teaching Strategies: An Experimental Project." Final report. Grand Forks: North Dakota University, Office of Education, Grant No. OEG-6-70-0039 (509), 1971 (51).

Barbara Mills. *Higher Level Thinking Abilities*. Portland: Northwest Regional Educational Laboratory, Report No. NREL-TR-6, 1971 (52).

Joel E. Bass. "The Development of an Inquiry Teaching Strategy and a Teachers' Training Module for Elementary Science." Final report. Huntsville, Texas: Sam Houston State College, Office of Education Grant No. OEC-6-71-0543 (509), 1972 (53).

Roada Wald. "The Effects of Models of Teaching as a Program for the Training of Teachers." Unpublished doctoral dissertation, Columbia University, 1972 (54).

Bruce R. Joyce, Marsha Weil, and Roada Wald. "The Teacher Innovator: Models of Teaching as the Core of Teacher Education." *Interchange* 4: 47-60; 1973 (55).

Annotation

Models of Teaching
Specific training in teaching strategies, using videomodeling and microteaching, was effective in increasing the number of strategies exhibited by student teachers.

Higher Level Thinking Strategies
A field test of the McCollum-Davis Model and the Duvall Model indicated that teachers learned concept formation strategies, interpretation of data, and application more efficiently when they were taught separately rather than in concert.

Inquiry Teaching Strategies
Use of a specially designed teachers' manual on inquiry skills for science teaching enabled student teachers to significantly improve their ability to identify inquiry behaviors on a paper and pencil test. Ability to use the behaviors was reported in terms of patterns of use one might expect for teacher trainees.

Models of Teaching
This study found no relationship between teacher trainees' natural teaching style and their acquisition of new models. Training resulted in the ability to demonstrate the models, but students returned to their normal style after completion of assigning teaching tasks. Ability to acquire a repertoire of teaching behaviors appeared to be a function of personal flexibility.

Models of Teaching
This report of a teacher education . program designed around the acquisition of models of teaching found conceptual level of teacher trainees to be positively related ($r = .420$) with the mastery of models.

6.
Developing a Repertoire of Models of Teaching

It does us little good to decide to achieve objectives and reach learners through a variety of methods unless we know that we can use them effectively. The question is invariably raised: "Can teachers learn a repertoire of models of teaching?" Over the last ten years, we have engaged in extensive research to develop methods that teachers can use to expand their repertoire. Much of this research has investigated the effects of instructional systems built around a strategy that presents the theory of a model first, demonstrates it as a whole, then breaks it down into its parts for practice, and concludes with exercises in which the teachers synthesize the parts of the model into a more complete clinical entity and apply it in the classroom.

Over a period of four years, a series of studies was planned and carried out with various populations of teachers and teacher candidates to determine whether, by means of these instructional systems, teachers could be brought to the point where they could practice models of teaching that required patterns of behavior considerably different from those that are normally observed in the classroom (O'Donnell (56), Wald (57), Weil (58), Murphy and Brown (59), Rude (60), Kelley (61), McKibbin (62), and Gower (63)). The vast variety of "natural" teaching styles contained considerable elements of what Hoetker and Albrand have so aptly described as a recitation style (64). This style is characterized by question-and-answer interchanges between teacher and student (chiefly teacher questions followed by student answers). O'Donnell's study used a very early version of the instructional system and demonstrated that teacher candidates learned patterns of behavior that were both relatively unusual classroom behaviors and that conformed to the theoretical specifications of the models of teaching to which they were exposed. Wald introduced

35

teacher candidates to models requiring not only patterns of behavior different from those that are "normal" in the classroom, but are very different from one another. Her candidates were exposed to a limited repertoire. Her study also demonstrated that the teacher candidates were able to produce, in the classroom, patterns of behavior that conformed to the theoretical specifications of the models and could produce them "on call." Nearly all of her students could, in other words, learn several models and apply them to classroom instruction. The power of the instructional systems was general—the models were learned equally well.

Wald also investigated the extent to which the normal teaching style of teachers influenced their acquisitions of the models. She correlated indices of teaching style with the clincial ratings of performance in the models and found no correlations in any area. In other words, normal teaching style did not influence the acquisition of the models of teaching. Teachers who normally displayed elements of particular models did not learn them any more completely than did those who rarely manifested those elements. (However, it should not be concluded that the normal style of a human being will not influence his/her ability to acquire a new frame of reference and act on it. The normal teaching styles of most teachers are extremely restricted, and stylistic differences occur over only a small part of the potential teaching spectrum. Therefore, we probably do not get *real* indicators of a teaching personality in the samples of behavior we normally encounter in the classroom. The restrictions on the role of the teacher, the kind of institution worked in, and the kinds of lessons normally taught greatly truncate the possibilities for the play of the teacher's personality on his/her transactions with children.)

Wald also studied the relationship between the educational and social values of teacher candidates and their preferences for various models. Except in one case, the social scale of the Allport-Vernon Study of Values, she found no relationships, but the relationship between the social scale and the acquisition of the most socially-oriented model of teaching was quite striking ($r > .60$).

Finally, Wald looked at the relationship between personality (*á la* Hunt) and the acquisition of teaching styles and determined that personal flexibility was not related to the acquisition of any one model of teaching, but was related to the acquisition of a variety of them. In other words, at least at the initial stages of training, the acquisition of repertory seemed to be a function of personal flexibility.

Wald advanced the following principles for us:

• Normal teaching styles contain few elements of most models of teaching.

• Teachers can learn a variety of models that they can use at will.

• Teaching style and, in most cases, personal values do not greatly interfere with training. An exception may be a relationship between social values and group-dynamics-oriented models.

When not practicing the models of teaching, her teachers generally returned to the modes of teaching that they displayed prior to training except when they chose to use a model. In other words, their new repertory could be displayed at will, but their old style remained in their repertoire.

The results of this work accord with that of McDonald, Allen, Orme (65), and their associates at Stanford during the middle 1960s, in which they demonstrated the ability to teach a repertoire of teaching skills through micro-teaching. Borg, Gall, Kelley, and their associates at the Far West Laboratory (66) also demonstrated that minicourses can be used to help teachers teach themselves complex teaching skills and strategies of a sort that are not ordinarily manifested in the classroom.

This work and theirs raises several questions about what is logically the first stage dependent variable in studies designed to influence teacher behavior. Wald and Weil's studies indicated very clearly that the teacher candidates who had been taught the repertory in models of teaching could manifest that repertory at will in the classroom and often did so on a voluntary basis as well as on call. However, when they were not practicing those models of teaching, their teaching behavior looked very much like that of any other group of teachers except they were somewhat less punishing than the average. In other words, if the dependent variable training was the acquisition of repertory, it was successful. But if the dependent variable was the teaching style of the teacher in general, then the training was not successful.

Many studies of teaching skills and many of the interaction analysis studies have had as their object the modification of the general teaching style of the teachers they were working with. In other words, having taught teachers a skill, such as a questioning technique, the investigator hoped the teachers would ask better questions all of the time. Or, having taught teachers to analyze their teaching, they hoped that more elements of teaching would pop up in their behavior.

It is our current belief that teaching style as a dependent variable is much less fruitful than is the demonstration of an acquired repertory that can be used at call. One reason for this is that it is not always clear when it is appropriate to use a teaching style. One might teach it to a teacher and then wait weeks before it was necessary for him/her to use it, or it might be weeks before it was both necessary for him/her to use it and there was also an observer present. If repertoire is the goal, however, one can as in the case of the McDonald, Allen, Orme studies, the Borg Meredith studies, and the Joyce, Wald, Weil studies, concentrate on the teacher's ability to produce skills of certain kinds when they are needed.

Skills in Models

Weil (67) approached the analysis of skills needed for models of teaching in several ways. First, she analyzed Wald's data and identified several types of behavior that teachers appeared to have difficulty mastering. She and Wald identified three teaching skills that they believed would have general facilitating power—they would boost across-model learning. She built instructional systems directed toward mastery of those skills and rated degrees of mastery in a group of teachers who were exposed to the skill training. She then exposed the teachers to a variety of models and correlated skill and model performance. The skills appeared to be model-specific resulting in the thesis that the more a model requires unusual teaching behavior, the more it requires additional skill-training in the "areas of unusualness."

Further Studies on the Acquisition of Models

Rude and Kelly (68) demonstrated that in-service teachers could acquire models at about the same rate as preservice teachers, and they and Gower extended the power of the clinical rating forms. Gower experimented with the use of videotape "exemplar" models of teaching as performance standards for novice teachers and worked out a system for comparing the interaction analysis profiles of teacher candidates with those of the "exemplar" episodes in order to identify the teaching skill discrepancies between the two groups. This should result in a far more precise description of the teaching skills relevant to each model than was previously the case.

Gower (69) found a significant correlation between degree of discrepancy between the pattern of teacher candidates and the "exemplar" patterns and the high-influence clinical rating forms embedded in the instructional systems, encouraging our use of somewhat more global analyses of teaching. Weil's intensive study of skill discrepancies (70) between teachers rated high and low in model performance has resulted also in an elaborated description of skills that were incorporated, with Gower's findings, into new instructional systems.

In subsequent work for the National Teacher Corps, a major component of the Summer Corpsmember Training Institute was developed to expose interns and experienced teachers in Teacher Corps to a repertoire of models.

The results of this work indicate that it is possible for teachers to acquire the capability to use a considerable variety of models provided that (a) they have time to become acquainted with the theory of the models; (b) they are demonstrated through videotape and live with children so that their features can be seen and understood; (c) that practice is provided with small groups of children in the skills necessary for carrying out each model; (d) feedback is provided to enable one to determine the success he/she is having in the areas in which he/she needs improvement; and (e) help is provided to determine the places within the curriculum where the variety of teaching approaches can be appropriately used.

Can teachers acquire a repertoire? The answer, so far, is "most can, with ease." Both pre- and in-service teachers appear to be able to acquire several models with relative ease, and normal patterns of teaching do not inhibit repertoire acquisition. Use of any given model subsequently depends on its selection for a given purpose or learner, which is as it should be.

7.
Designing Schools Around Distinctive Learning Experiences

Let us stretch our imaginations for a few pages and think of what we can do at a larger design level to create learning centers that provide the envelopes of learning experience for our students. Let us suppose that we combine the existence of our vast repertoire of teaching models with the power of multimedia informational and teaching systems.

To sharpen the issues, let us take a visit to a mythical school of the future, the design of which communicates the primary message of this paper. Our school is not housed within a single building. It is organized as a series of learning centers that occupy a variety of physical locations. These centers, which reflect the primary models of learning, are independently organized, although they share some technical support systems. In fact, a general storage and retrieval system is designed so that students can retrieve information and instructional systems in several media both from their homes and from the learning centers.

The learning centers are designed to serve several major purposes, which purposes give their names to the respective centers as follows: skills centers, academic centers, performing arts centers, social ecology centers, and idiosyncratic centers. Let us consider these centers in turn.

The Skills Center

The skills center employs diagnosticians who assess students' communications and other basic skills, and then refer them to appropriate instructional systems and to tutors. Whereas, the younger child spends considerable time in the skills center, persons of all ages return to the center to improve their old skills or learn new ones.

41

Communications skills in all media are included in the center. For example, making and viewing film is as prominent in the center as is writing and reading. At the advanced levels, seminars on form and substance, as well as training in the comparative analysis of media and symbol systems and their role in the culture, would be pursued.

The skills center would also include training in the use of the support systems that facilitate each of the learning systems. Training in the use of multimedia instructional systems, information storage and retrieval systems, and diagnostic and management systems is embedded in the center. The acquisition of these skills facilitates self-education and thereby complements the function of the idiosyncratic center.

Academic Centers

In the academic learning centers, devoted to the humanities, aesthetics, sciences, and mathematics, students join groups of other students for three types of courses. One type is survey courses in specific areas, conducted by teachers with support from the instructional systems center. These are followed by inquiry courses in which students ·work with academic teachers to try out the modes of inquiry of the disciplines. Advanced students relate to academic tutors who help them construct plans of personal study and to relate to groups of similarly advanced students. These centers are housed in laboratories that are especially constructed for the disciplines (as physics laboratories, art workshops, and so on) and are supported by the library and instructional systems centers in the same way as are the other centers.

The Performing Arts Centers

Music, drama, television and film production, dance, athletics, and the other performing arts are housed in a network of laboratories, workshops, and little theaters throughout the community. Students relate to the performing arts centers in a variety of ways, some for an initial survey experience, others for recreation, some for skill development, and others as a long-term, expressive venture.

The school contains other learning centers, but the number described thus far is probably sufficient to provide a concrete idea of the concept on which it is developed. The primary goal of such centers is the child's acquisition of a variety of models of learning that would serve as strategies in the child's further self-education. Matching models such as Hunt's (22) would be used by counselors to help students locate the learning models that would most facilitate their development. Learning centers and support systems would be always changing to meet emerging educational needs while maintaining the coherent, warm, and facilitative social system needed to provide stability to the student. Although a comprehensive design is still in the future, we have discussed some elements of such a design that can support a variety of educational means and ends.

The Social Ecology Centers

The social ecology center is devoted to the process of improving the society. It is organized to facilitate problem-solving groups who study social issues and problems, examine and improve their own interpersonal behavior, and generate social action to alleviate social problems and initiate improvements in societal relations.

The library, data bank, instructional systems centers, and the academic center provide support, but the social ecology center employs a series of simulators and an information retrieval system based on the "social situation of planet earth" as essential supports. An urban simulator supports the study of community problems, an internation simulator provides service to the study of international problems, and an "earth resources" simulator is used to study biological support systems.

The teachers in the social ecology centers are group leaders, for the most part, skilled in human relations training and the use of teaching models that facilitate dialogue on social problems and the organization of social action.

Students relate to the social ecology center from the earliest years, but at first they concentrate only on neighborhood problems and face-to-face human relations. Gradually they increase their scope, studying ecology, urbanization, government, and the creation of an international community. The simulators enable them to study social processes and to try alternative modes of social behavior. Human relations exercises help them to explore ways of reaching out to one another and organize themselves to improve social life in day-to-day relations and in the generation of action to improve societal patterns.

Idiosyncratic Centers

Idiosyncratic centers serve the students on their own terms. They are staffed with counselors and facilitators who relate to students as equals, helping them formulate their goals and procedures. The facilitators-teachers help the students relate to a wide variety of part-time teachers—members of the community who serve, largely on a voluntary basis, as tutors, resources, advisers, and teachers of short courses. In addition, they help students relate to the other centers where other teachers and tutors can serve them. The center for the performing arts, for example, serves individuals who wish to relate to activities in that center, as do the social ecology center and the academic study centers.

The idiosyncratic centers are also supported by a multimedia "library" and data bank, most of which is automated and which employs microfiche and microfiche copymaking units to give access to virtually all the material available in the Library of Congress. Many of the automated storage facilities are shared by all the schools of the region. The library supports all activities of the other centers.

The center is also supported by the instructional systems bank, which consists of an array of self-administering multimedia instructional systems in the most common areas. A modular plan permits students to select among the offerings and assemble sequences of them to serve specific purposes.

Thus, the idiosyncratic centers consist of counseling areas, where students (of all ages) make contact with counselors-facilitators who help them define their own goals and procedures and relate to the support services they need to achieve personal growth and enhanced individuality.

Teaching in Institutions

In our present schools, the teacher does the major selection in implementation of learning experiences. In the kind of school we have described in the last few pages the teaching role is built around the selection of particular kinds of educational missions and the models of teaching appropriate to them. This is a level of educational design that we have rarely engaged in in this country.

We have had innovative schools, to be sure, but most of them have been built around particular missions and goals. An educational system in a pluralistic society requires a more complex view of the learning experience. Theory and research and the development of instructional technology have given us the tools for this. If we can learn to plan schools around learning centers tailored for particular educational missions, we will have reached a new level of educational technology. Until then we can improve the selection of learning experiences by helping educational personnel become aware of the variety of theoretical alternatives in developing the clinical capacity to make them come alive in the classroom. In so doing, we can boost the probability that effective learning will take place and provide learners and teachers alike with a more delightful, interesting, and effective variety of opportunities for learning experiences.

References

1. For a description of a variety of approaches to teaching, see: Bruce Joyce and Marsha Weil. *Models of Teaching.* Englewood Cliffs, New Jersey: Prentice-Hall, Inc., 1972. Second edition in press for 1979; _____. *Social Models of Teaching.* Englewood Cliffs, New Jersey: Prentice-Hall, Inc., 1977; _____. *Personal Models of Teaching.* Englewood Cliffs, New Jersey: Prentice-Hall, Inc., 1977; _____. *Information-Processing Models of Teaching.* Englewood Cliffs, New Jersey: Prentice-Hall, Inc., 1977.

2. Herbert Thelen. *Education and the Human Quest.* New York: Harper & Row, 1960.

3. John Dewey. *Democracy and Education.* New York: Macmillan Publishing Co., Inc., 1916.

4. Byron Massialas and Benjamin Cox. *Inquiry in Social Studies.* New York: McGraw-Hill Book Co., 1966.

5. Kenneth Benne, Jack R. Gibb, and Leland Bradford. *T-Group Theory and Laboratory Method.* New York: John Wiley and Sons, Inc., 1964.

6. Donald Oliver and James P. Shaver. *Teaching Public Issues in the High School.* Boston: Houghton-Miffin Company, 1966.

7. Fannie Shaftel and George Shaftel. *Role-Playing for Social Values: Decision-Making in the Social Studies.* Englewood Cliffs, New Jersey: Prentice-Hall, Inc., 1967.

8. Sarene Boocock. *Simulating Games in Learning.* Beverly Hills, California: Sage Publications, 1968.

9. Hilda Taba. *Teacher's Handbook for Elementary Social Studies.* Reading, Massachusetts: Addison-Wesley Publishing Co., 1967.

10. Richard Suchman. *Inquiry Development Program: Developing Inquiry.* Chicago: Science Research Associates, 1966.

11. Joseph J. Schwab. *Biology Teachers' Handbook.* New York: John Wiley and Sons, Inc., 1963.

12. Jerome S. Bruner, Jacqueline J. Goodnow, and George A. Austin. *A Study of Thinking.* New York: Science Editions, Inc., 1967.

13. Jean Piaget. *The Origins of Intelligence in Children.* New York: International Universities Press, 1952.

14. Irving E. Sigel. "The Piagetian System and the World of Education." *Studies in Cognitive Development.* David Elkind and John Flavell, editors. New York: Oxford University Press, 1969.

15. Edmund Sullivan. "Piaget and the School Curriculum: A Critical Appraisal." Bulletin No. 2. Toronto: Ontario Institute for Studies in Education, 1967.

16. David Ausubel. *The Psychology of Meaningful Verbal Learning.* New York: Green and Stratton, 1963.

17. Harry Lorayne and Jerry Lucas. *The Memory Book.* New York: Ballantine Books, 1974.

18. Carl Rogers. *On Becoming a Person.* Boston: Houghton-Mifflin Company, 1951.

19. Fritz Perls, Ralph Hefferline, and Paul Goodman. *Gestalt Therapy: Excitement and Growth in the Human Personality.* New York: Crown Publishers, 1977.

20. William Schutz. *Joy: Expanding Human Awareness.* New York: Grove Press, 1967.

21. William Gordon. *Synectics.* New York: Harper & Row, 1961.

22. David E. Hunt. "A Conceptual Level Matching Model for Coordinating Learner Characteristics with Educational Approaches." *Interchange.* OISE Research Journal 1, June 1970.

23. William Glasser. *Schools Without Failure.* New York: Harper & Row, 1969.

24. B. F. Skinner. *The Science of Human Behavior.* New York: Macmillan Publishing Co., Inc., 1956.

25. David C. Rinn and John C. Masters. *Behavior Therapy: Techniques and Empirical Findings.* New York: Academic Press, 1974.

26. Joseph Wolpe and Andrew Lazarus. *Behavior Therapy Techniques: A Guide to the Treatment of Neuroses.* Oxford: Pergamon Publishers, 1966.

27. Harold Grietzkow *et al. Simulation in International Relations.* Englewood Cliffs, New Jersey: Prentice-Hall, Inc., 1963.

28. Robert Glaser, Julian Taber, and H. S. Halmuth. *Learning and Programmed Instruction.* Reading, Massachusetts: Addison-Wesley Publishing Co., Inc., 1965.

29. A. A. Lumsdaine. "Experimental Research on Instructional Devices and Materials." In: Robert Glaser, editor. *Training Research and Education.* Pittsburgh: University of Pittsburgh Press, 1962.

30. Skinner, *op. cit.*

31. See: Joyce and Weil. *Models of Teaching, op. cit.*

32. Gordon, *op. cit.*

33. Lee J. Cronbach and Richard Snow. *Aptitudes and Instructional Methods.* New York: Halsted Press, 1977.

34. David Hunt and Edmund Sullivan. *Between Psychology and Education.* New York: Holt, Rinehart and Winston, 1974.

35. Robert Spaulding. "Control of Deviancy in the Classroom as a Consequence of Ego-Enhancing Behavioral Management Techniques." *Journal of Research and Development in Education,* 1978 (in press); and M. R. Papageorgiou. *Observation of the Coping Behavior of Children in Elementary Schools.* San Jose, California: San Jose State University, 1977.

36. Ausubel, *op. cit.*

37. W. Timothy Gallwey. *The Inner Game of Tennis.* New York: Random House, 1974.

38. _____. *Inner Skiing.* New York: Random House, 1977.

Bruce Joyce, Booksend Laboratory,
Palo Alto, California.

ASCD Publications, Summer 1978

Yearbooks

Education for an Open Society (610-74012)	$8.00
Education for Peace: Focus on Mankind (610-17946)	$7.50
Evaluation as Feedback and Guide (610-17700)	$6.50
Feeling, Valuing, and the Art of Growing: Insights into the Affective (610-77104)	$9.75
Freedom, Bureaucracy, & Schooling (610-17508)	$6.50
Improving the Human Condition: A Curricular Response to Critical Realities (610-78132)	$9.75
Learning and Mental Health in the School (610-17674)	$5.00
Life Skills in School and Society (610-17786)	$5.50
A New Look at Progressive Education (610-17812)	$8.00
Perspectives on Curriculum Development 1776-1976 (610-76078)	$9.50
Schools in Search of Meaning (610-75044)	$8.50
Perceiving, Behaving, Becoming: A New Focus for Education (610-17278)	$5.00
To Nurture Humaneness: Commitment for the '70's (610-17810)	$6.00

Books and Booklets

About Learning Materials (611-78134)	$4.50
Action Learning: Student Community Service Projects (611-74018)	$2.50
Adventuring, Mastering, Associating: New Strategies for Teaching Children (611-76080)	$5.00
Beyond Jencks: The Myth of Equal Schooling (611-17928)	$2.00
The Changing Curriculum: Mathematics (611-17724)	$2.00
Criteria for Theories of Instruction (611-17756)	$2.00
Curricular Concerns in a Revolutionary Era (611-17852)	$6.00
Curriculum Leaders: Improving Their Influence (611-76084)	$4.00
Curriculum Theory (611-77112)	$7.00
Degrading the Grading Myths: A Primer of Alternatives to Grades and Marks (611-76082)	$6.00
Differentiated Staffing (611-17924)	$3.50
Discipline for Today's Children and Youth (611-17314)	$1.50
Educational Accountability: Beyond Behavioral Objectives (611-17856)	$2.50
Elementary School Mathematics: A Guide to Current Research (611-75056)	$5.00
Elementary School Science: A Guide to Current Research (611-17726)	$2.25
Eliminating Ethnic Bias in Instructional Materials: Comment and Bibliography (611-74020)	$3.25
Emerging Moral Dimensions in Society: Implications for Schooling (611-75052)	$3.75
Ethnic Modification of Curriculum (611-17832)	$1.00
Global Studies: Problems and Promises for Elementary Teachers (611-76086)	$4.50
Humanistic Education: Objectives and Assessment (611-78136)	$4.75
The Humanities and the Curriculum (611-17708)	$2.00
Impact of Decentralization on Curriculum: Selected Viewpoints (611-75050)	$3.75
Improving Educational Assessment & An Inventory of Measures of Affective Behavior (611-17804)	$4.50
International Dimension of Education (611-17816)	$2.25
Interpreting Language Arts Research for the Teacher (611-17846)	$4.00
Learning More About Learning (611-17310)	$2.00
Linguistics and the Classroom Teacher (611-17720)	$2.75
A Man for Tomorrow's World (611-17838)	$2.25
Middle School in the Making (611-74024)	$5.00
The Middle School We Need (611-75060)	$2.50
Multicultural Education: Commitments, Issues, and Applications (611-77108)	$7.00
Needs Assessment: A Focus for Curriculum Development (611-75048)	$4.00
Observational Methods in the Classroom (611-17948)	$3.50
Open Education: Critique and Assessment (611-75054)	$4.75
Open Schools for Children (611-17916)	$3.75
Professional Supervision for Professional Teachers (611-75046)	$4.50
Removing Barriers to Humaneness in the High School (611-17848)	$2.50
Reschooling Society: A Conceptual Model (611-17950)	$2.00
The School of the Future—NOW (611-17920)	$3.75
Schools Become Accountable: A PACT Approach (611-74016)	$3.50
The School's Role as Moral Authority (611-77110)	$4.50
Selecting Learning Experiences: Linking Theory and Practice (611-78138)	$4.75
Social Studies for the Evolving Individual (611-17952)	$3.00
Staff Development: Staff Liberation (611-77106)	$6.50
Supervision: Emerging Profession (611-17796)	$5.00
Supervision in a New Key (611-17926)	$2.50
Supervision: Perspectives and Propositions (611-17732)	$2.00
What Are the Sources of the Curriculum? (611-17522)	$1.50
Vitalizing the High School (611-74026)	$3.50
Developmental Characteristics of Children and Youth (wall chart) (611-75058)	$2.00

Discounts on quantity orders of same title to single address: 10-49 copies, 10%; 50 or more copies, 15%. Make checks or money orders payable to ASCD. Orders totaling $10.00 or less must be prepaid. Orders from institutions and businesses must be on official purchase order form. Shipping and handling charges will be added to billed purchase orders. **Please be sure to list the stock number of each publication, shown in parentheses.**

Subscription to **Educational Leadership**—$15.00 a year. ASCD Membership dues: Regular (subscription and yearbook)—$25.00 a year; Comprehensive (includes subscription and yearbook plus other books and booklets distributed during period of membership)—$35.00 a year.

Order from: **Association for Supervision and Curriculum Development Suite 1100, 1701 K Street, N.W., Washington, D.C. 20006**

39. Vic Braden and Bill Bruns. *Vic Braden's Tennis for the Future.* Boston: Little, Brown and Company, 1977.

40. See: Erich Fromm. *The Sane Society.* New York: Rinehart, 1955; Erich Fromm. *Escape from Freedom.* New York: Farrar and Rinehart, 1941; Erich Fromm. *The Art of Loving.* New York: Harper, 1956.

41. Calvin Taylor, editor. *Creativity: Progress and Potential.* New York: McGraw-Hill, 1964; Frank Barron. *Creativity and Psychological Health: Origins of Personal Vitality and Creative Freedom.* Princeton, New Jersey: Von Nostrand, 1963; E. Paul Torrance. *Gifted Children in the Classroom.* New York: Macmillan, 1965; Max Wertheimer *Productive Thinking.* New York: Harper, 1945.

42. Philip Phenix. *Education and the Common Good.* New York: Harper, 1961.

43. John Dewey. *Democracy and Education: An Introduction to the Philosophy of Education.* New York: Macmillan, 1946; John Dewey. *How We Think.* Boston: Heath, 1910; John Dewey. *The Child and the Curriculum* and *The School and Society.* Chicago: University of Chicago Press, 1960, 1956; John Dewey. *Reconstruction in Philosophy.* New York: Henry Holt, 1920; Henry G. Hullfish and Philip G. Smith. *Reflective Thinking: The Method of Education.* New York: Dodd, Mead, 1961.

44. David C. McClelland. *The Achievement Motive.* New York: Appleton-Century-Crofts, 1953; John W. Atkinson. *Achievement Motivation.* New York: Wiley, 1966; Carl Hansen. *Amidon.* Englewood Cliffs, New Jersey: Prentice-Hall, 1962.

45. Leonard S. Kenworthy. *Introducing Children to the World.* New York: Harper, 1955; Ralph C. Preston. *Improving the Teaching of World Affairs.* Englewood Cliffs, New Jersey: Prentice-Hall, 1956; The National Council for the Social Studies. *The Glens Falls Story* (Washington, D.C.: National Education Association, 1964) provides an interesting description of an entire community school's effort to carry out this objective.

46. See: Herbert A. Thelen. *Education and the Human Quest.* New York: Harper, 1961; Alice Miel and Peggy Brogan. *More Than Social Studies: A View of Social Learning in the Elementary School.* Englewood Cliffs, New Jersey: Prentice-Hall, 1957; John U. Michaelis. *Social Studies for Children in a Democracy.* Englewood Cliffs, New Jersey: Prentice-Hall, 1963.

47. William L. Shirer. *The Rise and Fall of the Third Reich.* New York: Simon and Schuster, 1960.

48. Muriel Crosby. *An Adventure in Human Relations.* Chicago: Follett, 1965; Fannie R. Shaftel and George Shaftel. *Role-Playing for Social Values: Decision-Making in the Social Studies.* Englewood Cliffs, New Jersey: Prentice-Hall, 1967; Hilda Taba. *Thinking in Elementary School Children.* San Francisco: San Francisco State College, 1964; Hilda Taba. *Intergroup Education in Public Schools.* Washington, D.C.: American Council on Education, 1952; Lloyd and Elaine Cook. *School Problems in Human Relations.* New York: McGraw-Hill, 1957; Lloyd and Elaine Cook. *Intergroup Education.* New York: McGraw-Hill, 1954.

49. Lucy Sprague Mitchell. *Our Children and Our Schools.* New York: Simon and Schuster, 1950.

50. O. J. Harvey, David E. Hunt, and Harold M. Schroder. *Conceptual Systems and Personality Organization.* New York: John Wiley and Sons, Inc., 1961.

51. Patricia D. Murphy. "Training in Teaching Strategies: An Experimental Project." Final report. Grand Forks: North Dakota University, Office of Education, Grant No. OEG-6-70-0039 (509), 1971.

52. Barbara Mills. *Higher Level Thinking Abilities.* Portland: Northwest Regional Educational Laboratory, Report No. NREL-TR-6, 1971.

53. Joel E. Bass. "The Development of an Inquiry Teaching Strategy and a Teachers' Training Module for Elementary Science." Final report. Huntsville, Texas: Sam Houston State College, Office of Education Grant No. OEC-6-71-0543 (509), 1972.

54. Roada Wald. "The Effects of Models of Teaching as a Program for the Training of Teachers." Unpublished doctoral disertation, Columbia University, 1972.

55. Bruce R. Joyce, Marsha Weil, and Roada Wald. "The Teacher Innovator: Models of Teaching as the Core of Teacher Education." *Interchange* 4: 47-60, 1973.

56. Katherine O'Donnell. "Natural Teaching Styles and Modes of Teaching: The Production of Classroom-Unusual Teaching Behavior." Unpublished doctoral dissertation, Columbia University, 1974.

57. Roada Wald, *op. cit.*

58. Marsha Weil. "Deriving Teaching Skills from Models of Teaching." See: R. Houston, editor. *Assessment in Competency-Based Teacher Education.* San Francisco: McCutchan Publishing Corp., 1974.

59. P. D. Murphy and M. M. Brown. "Conceptual Systems and Teaching Styles." *American Educational Research Journal,* 1970.

60. Eugene Rude. "The Analysis of the Intersection Patterns Characteristic of Phases of Models of Teaching." Unpublished doctoral dissertation, Columbia University, 1973.

61. George A. Kelly. *The Psychology of Personal Constructs.* New York: Norton & Co., Inc., 1955.

62. Michael McKibbin. "The Application of Three Instruction Analysis Systems to Investigate Models of Teaching." Unpublished doctoral dissertation, Columbia University, 1974.

63. Robert Gower. "The Use of an Exemplary Teaching Profile to Assess Teaching Performance in an Induction Model." Unpublished doctoral dissertation, Columbia University, 1974.

64. James Hoetker and William Albrand. "The Persistence of the Recitation." *American Educational Research Journal* 6: March 1969.

65. F. J. McDonald, D. Allen, and M. Orme. "Experiment II: Effects of Feedback and Practice Conditions on the Acquisition of a Teaching Strategy." Stanford, California: Stanford University, 1966.

66. W. Borg, G. Meredith, M. Kelley, and P. Langer. "The Minicourse: A Microteaching Approach to Teacher Education." Beverly Hills, California: Collier-Macmillan Educational Services, 1970.

67. Weil, *op. cit.*

68. Rude and Kelly, *op. cit.*

69. Gower, *op. cit.*

70. Weil, *op. cit.*

Contents

ACKNOWLEDGMENTS

Final editing of the manuscript and publication of this booklet were the responsibility of Robert R. Leeper, Associate Director and Editor, ASCD Publications. The production was handled by Patricia Connors, Editorial Assistant, with the assistance of Nancy Olson, Myra Taub, Elsa Angell, and Teola T. Jones. The author would also like to thank Pat Phelan, who helped make this book possible.